FIESTA!

SRI LANKA

GROLIER

An Imprint of Scholastic Library Publishing
Danbury, Connecticut

Published for Grolier
an imprint of Scholastic Library Publishing
Old Sherman Turnpike, Danbury, Connecticut 06816
by Marshall Cavendish Editions
an imprint of Marshall Cavendish International
1 New Industrial Road, Singapore 536196

Set ISBN: 0-7172-5788-6
Volume ISBN: 0-7172-5801-7

Library of Congress Cataloging-in-Publication Data
Sri Lanka.
p. cm.—(Fiesta!)
Summary: Discusses the festivals and holidays of Sri Lanka and how the songs, food,
and traditions associated with these celebrations reflect the culture of the people.
1. Festivals—Sri Lanka—Juvenile literature. 2. Sri Lanka—Social life and customs—Juvenile literature.
[1. Festivals—Sri Lanka. 2. Holidays—Sri Lanka. 3. Sri Lanka—Social life and customs.]
I. Grolier (Firm). II. Fiesta! (Danbury, Conn.)
GT4876.2.A2A75 2004
394.265493—dc21   2003044851

For this volume
Author: Leena Ng
Editor: Yeo Puay Khoon
Designer: Jailani Basari
Production: Nor Sidah Haron
Crafts and Recipes produced by Stephen Russell

Printed by Everbest Printing Co. Ltd

Adult supervision advised for all crafts and recipes,
particularly those involving sharp instruments and heat.

CONTENTS

SRI LANKA

The island of Sri Lanka appears as a tiny spot in the Indian Ocean on the world map. In reality the tropical isle is a beautiful and colorful mixture of religions, cultures, landmarks, and geography.

▼ **Adam's Peak,** also called Sri Pada, is Sri Lanka's most sacred mountain. People of all faiths congregate at this site to pay respects to the giant footprint found at the summit. Muslims believe it was left behind by Adam. Buddhists claim it was Buddha's footprint, while Hindus claim it was a mark of Shiva.

GULF OF MANNAR

▲ **The Fort** is a landmark in the capital city of Colombo. Built in 1857 during the British occupation, it is the only lighthouse in the world located away from the beach in a city center. The home of Sri Lanka's president and the Old Parliament House both stand next to the Fort.

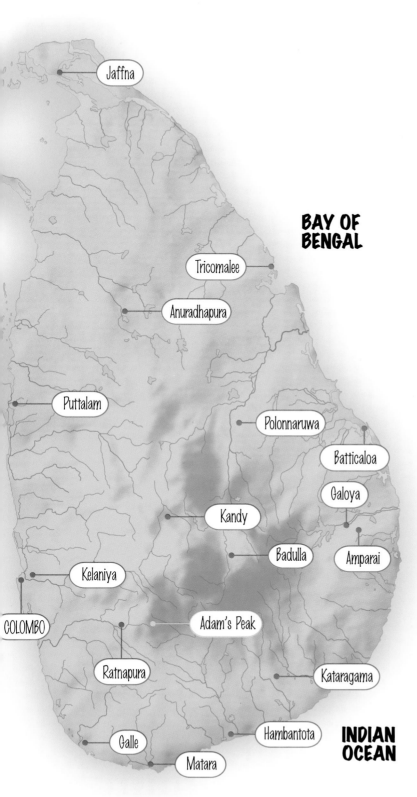

Jaffna

BAY OF
BENGAL

Tricomalee

Anuradhapura

Puttalam

Polonnaruwa

Batticaloa

Galoya

Kandy

Badulla

Amparai

Kelaniya

COLOMBO

Adam's Peak

Ratnapura

Kataragama

Galle

Hambantota

Matara

INDIAN
OCEAN

▼ **Kandyan Dance** is the national dance of Sri Lanka. The movements in this unique dance are based on words taken from the *Ramayana*, which is a Hindu poem that tells the story of Lord Rama.

▼ **The Sinharaja Rainforest** in the southwest lowlands of Sri Lanka is one of few remaining forests of its kind in Asia. Elephants, monkeys, and many other creatures live in the forest and are allowed to roam freely. The rainforest is also home to over 170 kinds of orchids.

RELIGIONS

Sri Lanka celebrates many colorful national and religious festivals. Hardly a month goes by without a celebration happening in a city or town. Sometimes, several festivities even take place in different parts of the country at the same time!

Shiva, the God of Destruction, is one of the gods in Hinduism.

SRI LANKANS are made up of four main groups of people: Sinhala, Tamil, Moor, and Burgher. The Sinhala make up the largest group, and most Sinhalese are devout Buddhists.

Buddhism was first introduced to the island by Mahinda. His father, the great Indian Emperor Ashoka, was a Buddhist who sent missions all around the Indian continent. Buddhism took a strong hold on the country very quickly, and Sri Lanka became a center for Buddhist teachings.

In fact, the recorded history of Sri Lanka began only when Buddhism gave

birth to a cultural revolution more than two thousand years ago. The religion has since shaped Sri Lanka, as it fostered the arts and led to the setting up of statues, temples, monasteries, irrigation systems, and reservoirs.

Buddhism is still preserved in its purest form by its followers today. Buddha statues and stupas, or monuments, can be found throughout Sri Lanka. Its teaching of peace and tolerance has left a gentle mark on the people.

Hinduism is Sri Lanka's second most important religion and is mostly practiced by Tamils. Legend has it that Tamil kings and their followers from south India brought Hinduism to Sri Lanka. Today, there are large Hindu communities in the capital Colombo, Kandy, and the tea plantation areas in the hill country, as well as in the northern and eastern parts of the island. Although Hindu beliefs and practices vary from region to region, there are some similarities among them. They include common beliefs in reincarnation, destiny, appropriate behavior, and the caste system.

A Catholic decorative piece depicting the Virgin Mary and baby Christ.

Early visitors to Sri Lanka also brought with them the practices and beliefs of their religions. For example, Arab traders introduced Islam in the eight century, while Portuguese colonizers brought Roman Catholicism in the sixteenth century. Today, the Catholic Church remains strong among the western coastal communities in Sri Lanka, as shown by the many churches in these areas.

GREETINGS FROM **SRI LANKA!**

It is easy to get by in Sri Lanka with English, which is spoken among the different groups of people in the vast country. Sinhala and Tamil are the two national languages of Sri Lanka and are spoken interchangeably even between the Sinhalese and Tamils themselves. Sri Lankans are friendly people and generally offer greetings to everyone, even strangers. In the countryside English is not so common, so it is helpful to speak a few words of Sinhala or Tamil.

How do you say...

Hello
Ayubowan

Goodbye
Ayubowan ge hilla ennam

Thank you
Sthuthiy

My name is...
Mage nama...

How are you?
Kohomadha?

THAI PONGAL

Thai Pongal is a harvest festival held in honor of the Sun God. Just like Thanksgiving, families rejoice and share the joy of their harvests with others during this time.

Newly harvested rice with milk is boiled in earthen pots.

Thai Pongal is celebrated in Sri Lanka on January 14 to coincide with the harvest season. Farmers originally saw Thai Pongal as a day to give thanks for their bountiful harvests and livestock. Over time other groups of people also recognized the occasion, and the festival is now celebrated by all Hindus.

Pongal is the Tamil word for a sweet porridge of rice and milk. After praying at a Hindu temple, every household boils a large pot of newly harvested rice cooked in spicy, sweetened milk. The pot is purposely left to boil over since this spillover of milk is a symbol of abundance and indicates good luck for the new year. Sometimes, firecrackers are also set off. Once the pongal is ready, an offering is made to the Sun God before the dish is shared among family and friends.

There is excitement and much preparation for the festival. New clothes are made or bought for everyone in the family. Homes are cleaned, and feasts, which include the Sri Lankan staple dish of hoppers, are prepared.

On the day of Pongal people wake up early and bathe themselves to wash away any bad luck. They then visit temples where

Candle lamps are lighted and placed around the overflowing earthen pot during Thai Pongal.

Kolam patterns are made to beautify the house during the festive occasion.

religious ceremonies are performed. Family members gather at the courtyards of their homes to draw beautiful designs, or *kolam*, using rice flour and turmeric. At the center of this kolam, a new earthen pot with water is kept on the hearth, and the pongal is cooked. Oil lamps are also lighted and kept beside it.

Love and peace are the central theme of Thai Pongal, which is also a day for family members to reunite and for friends to get together. Quarrels are forgotten as people make up and get over their differences.

HOPPERS

SERVES 4

Yeast mixture:
2 tbsp yeast granules
1 tbsp sugar
1/8 cup lukewarm water

4 cups rice flour
2 cups lukewarm water
13 oz can of coconut milk diluted with 1/2 can of lukewarm water
2 tbsp sugar
1 tbsp oil

1 Mix together the ingredients for the yeast mixture, and leave for 15 minutes until it becomes frothy.

2 Put the rice flour into a large bowl, and add the yeast mixture, followed by the lukewarm water. Mix well. Cover the bowl with a damp cloth or plastic wrap, and leave for about eight hours in a warm place. The batter should rise to double the original amount.

3 Add 3/4 of the coconut milk mixture and the sugar to the batter. Stir well. If more liquid is needed, add the remainder of the coconut mix little by little. The batter should be thinner than a pancake batter.

4 Soak a small piece of cloth in a saucer of oil. Heat a small wok on medium heat for 3 minutes. When it is hot, rub the pan thoroughly with the oiled cloth. (Ask an adult to help you.) Add about 1/4 cup of the batter to the pan, and turn the pan in a circular motion so that the batter sticks to the sides of the pan.

5 Cover and cook for about 1 minute over low-medium heat. Use a butter knife to loosen the edges of the hopper, and serve hot, preferably with some brown sugar.

INDEPENDENCE DAY

On February 4, 1948, Ceylon (as Sri Lanka was then known) gained independence from Britain. The country was once again ruled by its own people. This day is celebrated with pomp and pageantry.

Independence Day is a great patriotic national occasion. This day is marked with colorful parades in Colombo, the capital city. The country's achievement of independence after 133 years under British rule is seen as a major event by the people.

In 1948 on the first Independence Day people across the country raised the 2,000-year-old Lion Flag to display their pride in ruling their own land once again. Considered the oldest national flag in the world, the Lion Flag signified justice, harmony, peace, and prosperity to everyone. Before long, it was recognized by almost all communities in the country as the national flag of the free Sri Lanka.

Since then the Lion Flag has become one of the best-selling articles in shops in all major cities in Sri Lanka. As early as January every year, people of all walks of life, from humble hut dwellers to wealthy professionals, fly it from their rooftops in preparation for the grand celebrations.

Elaborately dressed elephants are paraded in public processions to celebrate the occasion.

A number of cultural and religious activities take place throughout the country. Parades, pageants, and traditional dances showcase the nation's culture and achievements.

Processions of richly adorned elephants and parades involving dancers and drummers from all around the island are held to display Sri Lanka's traditional forms of art.

Cricket, the national game of Sri Lanka, is played on Independence Day to celebrate the nation's success in the sport.

SRI LANKA NATIONAL ANTHEM

S - ri   Lanka   Ma - tha,

A - pa   S - ri Lan - ka,

Na - mo   Na - mo

Na - mo   Na - mo Ma - tha,

Sunda-ra   si - ri   ba - ri - ni,

surandi athi   soba mana Lan - ka

Dhanya dhanaya neka mal palathuru piri,

ja - ya   bhoomi - ya Ram - ya

Mother Lanka — we salute Thee!
Plenteous in prosperity, Thou,
Beauteous in grace and love,
Laden with corn and luscious fruit
And fragrant flowers of radiant hue,
Giver of life and all good things.

THE STORY OF CEYLON TEA

Blessed with ideal climatic conditions for growing tea,
Sri Lanka has been producing Ceylon tea of the highest quality since 1867.
Today, tea is Sri Lanka's most important industry.

CEYLON TEA FROM Sri Lanka has been acclaimed as the best tea in the world for more than a century. The country's good climate and fertile soil produce a unique flavor and aroma found only in Ceylon tea.

Tea, however, is said to have been discovered by accident in ancient China. The Chinese believe that it was Emperor Shen-Nung who first tasted tea in 2737 B.C. The story goes that while he was boiling some drinking water in the garden, a few leaves from a wild tea bush flew into the pot. The emperor liked the delicate flavor that the leaves gave to his water so much that he introduced the art of tea making to the Chinese people.

In 1867 a British planter named James Taylor introduced tea plants to Sri Lanka to replace the coffee crops that had been affected by disease. Since then tea has become a popular plantation crop. It is grown not only on the hilly slopes of Sri Lanka's central highlands but also at mid and low elevations.

However, it was not until 23 years later that Sir Thomas J. Lipton — the British businessman behind the now famous Lipton tea brand — bought his first estates in Ceylon. Since then tea, especially Lipton tea, has become synonymous with Sri Lanka the world over.

The first estates Sir Thomas acquired in Ceylon were in Haputale, which included the plantations of Dambatenne, Laymostotte, and Monerakande. The Dambatenne Estate was approximately

130 miles from Colombo. Measuring two to three thousand acres, the estate was Sir Thomas's favorite home in Sri Lanka. He is said to have had a favorite chair that he frequently sat in to relax and enjoy the scenic beauty of the hill country. This "Lipton's Seat," as it is known, can still be seen at the estate. From this seat set at an altitude of 6,430 feet tourists can enjoy a breathtaking view of the southeastern part of the country — just as the famous tea planter did over a century ago.

SINHALA NEW YEAR

Sinhala New Year, or Sinhala Aluth Avurudu, signifies the beginning of the New Year for both Buddhists and Hindus. Folk dances, national games, and customs are revived during this period of peace and love.

T he people of Sri Lanka recognize two separate new years. In January they celebrate the conventional New Year, and in the second week of April they celebrate the Sinhala New Year.

This traditional New Year is the most important festival of the Sinhala and Tamil people of Sri Lanka. Many time-honored customs are observed at favorable times that are determined by astrologers. Festivities continue for about a week, with festivals held all over the country.

There is a festive air as preparations for the event begin as early as March, when all members of the family go shopping for new clothes.

An oil lamp must always be lighted before having the first meal of the New Year.

Houses are thoroughly cleaned and sometimes even whitewashed and given a new coat of paint. Special food items are also stored for entertaining friends and relatives during the long holiday. People also have their horoscopes read.

Brass pots are washed and cleaned before the arrival of the New Year.

14

The most important task in food preparation is the making of oil cakes and sweetmeats, such as *kokis, aluwa,* and *aggala.* The traditional practice is to make them at home, although they are now readily available at shops and supermarkets.

Astrologers provide an exact time to stop all work for the old year, called *parana avurudda* in Tamil. Before this time the last meal of the year is eaten, and pots and pans washed. The hearth is also cleaned and the floors washed. Even the last bath is taken before the year ends.

NIL AHAS THALE

C F Dm

Nil ahas thale agei - Ne wala kulu -

C G

Lassanai pura hande - Ras vihidila -

Am G Dm

Nil nelum nida vate - Manel mal pipi -

G G₇ C

Lassanai pura hande - Ras vihidila

A quiet period, or *nogathaya*, is duly observed before the arrival of the New Year. Nogathaya is a time reserved for religious activity, but children are allowed to play. Nogathaya can last for several hours, during which no food is eaten, and no serious work is done.

When the New Year arrives, the mother of the household, dressed in new clothes with the lucky colors picked out for her, lights the hearth. She will do this at the precise time set by astrologers and in the proper direction. A pot of milk and rice is boiled in a new clay pot and allowed to spill over. Firecrackers are set off at this moment, creating a joyful din in the entire neighborhood.

The head of each household then feeds each member of the house a mouthful of milk rice in a ritual that calls for peace in the family. Tables are laid with a vast variety of foods, many of which are cooked only during this special holiday.

Children especially enjoy Aluth Avurudu because they are given cash gifts wrapped in betel leaves by the adults. Money is also exchanged among families and friends in a tradition known as *ganu denu*.

Many people take the time to visit relatives and friends and get over their old grievances during the New Year.

Traditional games, such as climbing greased poles, pillow fights, or *kotta pora*, *raben*, or drum contests, and *gudu*, a field game similar to baseball, are played by people of all ages. *Olinda*, a board game like backgammon, is also played indoors using a special board.

Traditionally, festive candies are made at home and served to friends and relatives when they visit. Flowers such as lotuses are used to decorate the house.

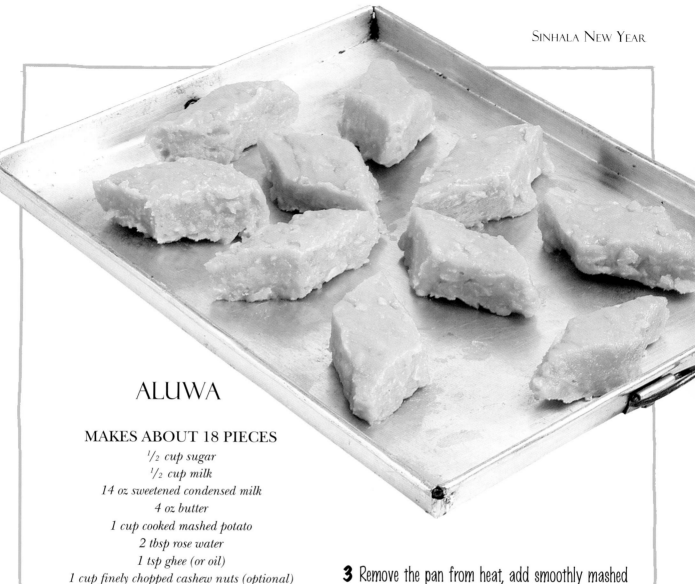

ALUWA

MAKES ABOUT 18 PIECES

¹/₂ cup sugar
¹/₂ cup milk
14 oz sweetened condensed milk
4 oz butter
1 cup cooked mashed potato
2 tbsp rose water
1 tsp ghee (or oil)
1 cup finely chopped cashew nuts (optional)
1 tsp ground cardamom (optional)

1 Put sugar, milk, condensed milk, and ghee into a large, heated nonstick pan.

2 Cook over medium heat, stirring constantly until mixture is reduced to a paste. To test if it is ready, drop a little into a cup of ice-cold water. If it is firm enough to be molded into a soft ball, it has reached the right temperature.

3 Remove the pan from heat, add smoothly mashed potato, and mix with a beater until all lumps are smoothed out.

4 Return the pan to heat, and cook to a paste once more. Remove from heat, stir in nuts, rose water, and cardamom. Mix well.

5 Pour into a well buttered shallow dish or baking pan. Press lightly with a piece of buttered aluminum foil to smoothe and flatten the surface. Allow to cool and set, then cut into diamond shapes for serving.

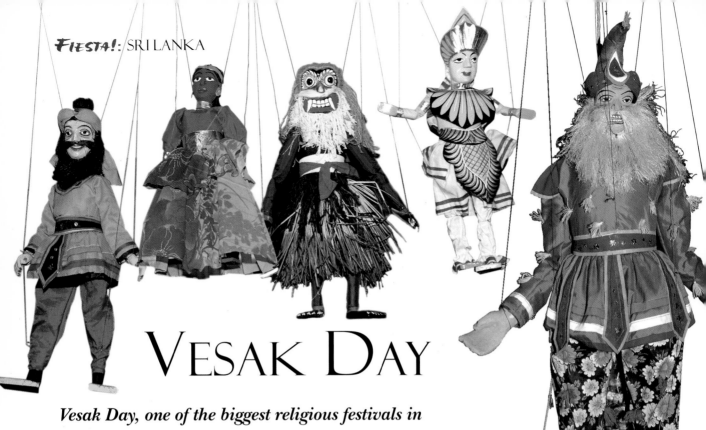

VESAK DAY

Vesak Day, one of the biggest religious festivals in Sri Lanka, is also celebrated by Buddhists around the world. It is a sacred day for commemorating the birth, enlightenment, and passing away of Buddha.

Puppet shows are staged as entertainment on the evening of Vesak Day.

The Buddhist year begins with the month of Vesak in May. It is believed that Lord Buddha was born, attained the state of enlightenment, and passed away all on the full moon of the month.

Nirvana, or the state of enlightenment, is reached when one completely understands the nature of life. So, Vesak is often called the "Thrice Blessed Day." Legend also has it that it was on this day that Buddha made his third and final visit to Sri Lanka during the eighth year of his enlightenment.

Buddhists mark this sacred full moon festival with countless religious observations, including the observation of the *dharma* (preachings of Buddha). Besides making offerings of flowers to the relics and statues of Lord Buddha, devotees also pay homage to the deity by lighting various types of lanterns and *pandals*, or tent houses.

Vesak Day is a festival of lights and color. The temples come alive with huge, illuminated pandals showing varied scenes from Buddha's life. Thousands of electric jets throwing brilliant color patterns are set up in the city to add to the spirit of the occasion. A large number of colored lanterns turn the towns and villages into a dream world.

Buddhists decorate their homes with oil lamps and lanterns known as vesak buckets. Nights are the happiest times for children as they go out with their parents to view the lights and decorations. And they get to show off their colorful lanterns in the streets on their way to the temple. Puppet shows and theater performances are specially staged on this day. Since it is considered good to offer food and drink during Vesak Day, roads are dotted with booths, or *dansals*, offering free food and drinks to passersby.

MAKE YOUR OWN PAPER LANTERN

YOU WILL NEED

1 sheet of paper
Glue or tape
Crayons, markers, or poster paints
Long string
2 craft or popsicle sticks
1 thin, medium-length stick

1 Paint or draw some simple patterns on one side of the paper.

2 Roll the paper into a cyclinder, with the two shorter sides meeting each other. Overlap one end over the other, and glue or tape it down to hold its shape.

3 Flatten one end of the cyclinder, and make a fold. Seal the fold with glue or tape, and then make two markings on the fold.

4 Use strong glue to secure the two craft or popsicle sticks together to form an X. Align the sticks so that the X is at the center of one end of the lantern opposite the pen markings. Shave off the edges that stick out, so that the sticks can be glued on securely just inside the end of the lantern.

5 Punch out two small holes at the markings on the top of the lantern, and tie the string at both ends. The string should be neither too taut nor too slack, but just long enough to act as a handle for the lantern to be carried.

6 Wind the stick around the string, so that the lantern hangs on one end of it.

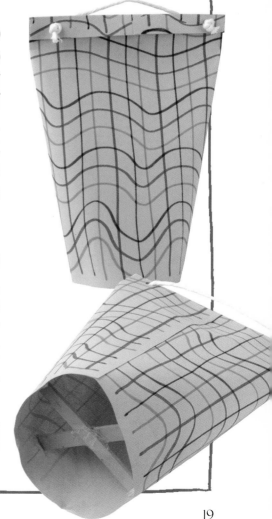

KANDY ESALA PERAHERA

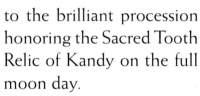

This event pays homage to Buddha with many colorful and spectacular pageants leading up to the climax on the day of the full moon.

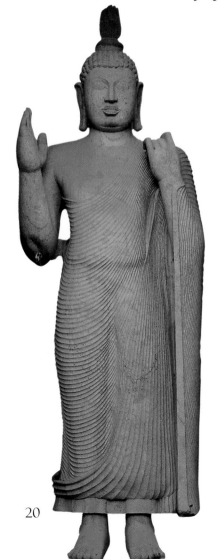

Esala, or the months of July and August, is the season of festivals, with the day of the full moon being the climax of some of these festivals.

The most magnificent of these religious holidays is Kandy Esala Perahera, held over 10 days in the hill city of Kandy. This string of *peraheras*, or processions, is hailed with torchbearers, whip-crackers, dancers, and elephants. Each day the procession increases in pageantry in the buildup

The precious Tooth Relic of Buddha is the centerpiece of Kandy Esala Perahera.

to the brilliant procession honoring the Sacred Tooth Relic of Kandy on the full moon day.

According to folklore, there are Four Tooth Relics of Buddha. One of them came into the possession of King Brahmadatta of Dantupura, known as Orissa in India today. On King Brahmadatta's death his son Prince Guhasiva became king. But it was not long before the king's enemies began waging a war against Guhasiva to take over his kingdom.

Guhasiva, fearing that the precious Tooth Relic

would be stolen, directed Prince Danta to take it to Sri Lanka for safekeeping. Prince Danta fled to safety, carrying the Sacred Tooth Relic with him. From then on, the relic became a national treasure of Sri Lanka, and it was kept in different parts of the country until King Vimaladharmasuriya, the second-to-last king of Kandy, put it in the Temple of the Sacred Tooth Relic.

During the procession a golden casket containing the Sacred Tooth Relic is carried by the Maligawa Tusker, a magnificent looking elephant, through the streets of Kandy.

Thousands of temple chieftains, acrobats, pipers, drummers, trumpeters, performers wearing kolam masks, torchbearers, and whip-crackers all add to the excitement. There are also hundreds of elephants dressed in silks and colored lights that are allowed to stroll just a few feet from the huge crowd. The celebration carries on late into the night, making the Kandy Esala a truly unforgettable experience.

MAKE YOUR OWN KOLAM MASK

YOU WILL NEED
2 paper plates
Crayons and markers
Paintbrushes and poster colors
Glue
Strings
Wooden stick
Crepe paper (optional)

1 Use one paper plate as the main "face" of your mask.

2 Decorate your mask with bright colors using crayons, markers, or poster paints.

3 Cut out two holes for the eyes and a slit for the mouth. Cut a pyramid-shaped nose and two ears from the second paper plate, and glue them onto your mask. You can add strips of crepe paper to decorate the mask.

4 Glue the stick to the center of the mask so that you can hold up the mask in front of your face.

THE DANCE
TO WARD OFF EVIL

Sri Lankans believe that by performing the devil dance, evil spirits and diseases can be driven away, and good spirits will give their blessings.

SRI LANKA'S FAMOUS devil dance may have its origins in South India. But the traditional ritual often performed at religious festivals, especially the Kataragama Festival, has developed a local character.

Devil dancing is generally performed to free a person from demons, evil spirits, or just plain bad luck. The dance was very popular in the past decade. Unfortunately, the high costs of staging these dances and the modernization of these old cultural practices mean that they are taking place less often these days.

Typically, a devil dance consists of three parts, those of demons, deities, and semidemons. Before the dance begins, palm-leafed shrines are built outside a person's house. The male dancers spin continuously, with a white cloth wound tightly round their hips and a red cloth tied around their heads with strips of palm leaves hanging down from it. All this takes place while bare-chested drummers beat out frantic rhythms on a double-sided, cylindrical drum. From time to time there is a break in the dancing when other participants perform mimes and magic. At the climax of the routine dancers put on masks representing the demons and act out a scene explaining who they are and why they have entered a victim's body to inflict distress or a disease on him. The chief exorcist then questions and threatens the demon, and tells it to leave. Sometimes, he may even try to bribe the demon to go away.

There are many types of devil dances.

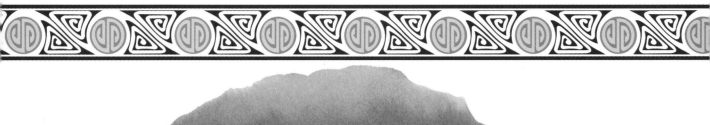

One dance, the *sanni yakku*, is performed to get rid of a disease-causing demon, which is represented by a range of characters including a pregnant woman and a mother. Other dances include the *kohomba kankariya*, which is performed to ensure prosperity, and the *bali*, which is performed to appease the heavenly beings.

KATARAGAMA FESTIVAL

The Kataragama Festival has great importance in Sri Lanka. People from all over the country and of all religions gather in the town of Kataragama to fulfill their vows or to seek knowledge and guidance from the gods.

Devotees wear the devil dance mask while performing the dance to seek blessings from the gods.

Kataragama, a city located in the southeastern part of Sri Lanka, is a popular destination for both Buddhist and Hindu pilgrims.

The main event at the town is the Kataragama Festival, which is held for two weeks from July to August every year.

Followers of Hinduism and Buddhism perform various rituals, such as doing the devil dance, to seek blessings from the gods or to repay the kindness that has been given them. Some people also perform more daring rituals such as rolling themselves on scorching sand, walking barefoot over hot coals, and piercing their tongues with skewers.

According to Hindu mythology, the gods were at one time enslaved by the ungodly forces, and they appealed to Lord Shiva for assistance. The mighty Shiva then sent his second son, Skanda, to lead the army of the gods to a victory against evil. On his way back Skanda stopped at Kataragama and met a lovely woman called Valli Amma. Skanda later made Valli his second wife. A shrine, the Kataragama Devale, was built in the town and dedicated to this romantic legend.

The highlight of the festival is the two-week-long procession that takes place every night. Long before the set hour, the temple grounds are filled with believers balancing earthen jars of holy ash and burning camphor and people playing drums and flutes. Amid all this noise and commotion temple officials put up a *yantra*, or casket with a diagram of Lord Skanda, on the back of an elephant. The procession then moves at a slow pace amid the beat of drums, moaning of conches, tinkling of bells, and cries of the pilgrims gathered there. The perahera ends with a water ceremony, when the yantra is purified again by dipping it in water.

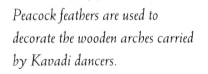

Peacock feathers are used to decorate the wooden arches carried by Kavadi dancers.

Another popular attraction is the exciting fire-walking ceremony, held a few days before the end of the festival. Following a procession of elephants and Kavadi dancers who carry wooden arches decorated with peacock feathers, devotees receive their blessings in the waters of a sacred river before dancing to a tremendous burst of drum beats and onto a bed of red-hot embers. The spectators become intensely excited when everyone emerges unhurt despite their bare feet. Through the years this fire-walking ceremony has still retained its symbolic association with ancient fertility rites.

VEL FESTIVAL

This event is celebrated by Hindu Tamils in different parts of the country. The most elaborate festivities are held in Colombo. Replicas of Lord Skanda are paraded in the Vel Chariot for the processions.

The main streets of Colombo take on a festival atmosphere in August every year when the capital's main Hindu festival, Vel, takes place. Born out of the Kataragama Festival, the Vel Festival became a tradition of the island only in 1874, when a cholera epidemic prevented the people from making pilgrimages to Kataragama.

As a result, the wealthy south Indian business community in Colombo decided to stage its own event. Ever since then the Vel Festival has been a national holiday to honor the War God, Lord Skanda.

On the last night of the Kataragama Festival a procession of *Kavadis*, or decorated wooden arches,

Colorful lanterns made of fabric are hung up as decorations for celebrating the Vel Festival.

Various groups of dancers join lavishly dressed elephants in the joyous carnival.

leaves the Skanda Temple in the main street of Colombo for the Skanda Temple in Wellawatte.

On the following day the Vel procession, symbolically carrying the *vel*, or spear, with which Lord Skanda is said to have defeated the ungodly powers, leaves the Skanda Temple in Sea Street and is ceremoniously hauled to another Skanda Temple in Bambalapitiya. These trips symbolically represent the union of Lord Skanda and his partner Valli. All ceremonies take place at the Bambalapitiya temple and Wellawatte temple over the next three days.

Great importance is attached to the Vel Festival by the people of Sri Lanka. The Vel Chariot, or festival wagon, is magnificently carved and gilded to bear the weapons of the Hindu God of War. It is always drawn by two strong white bulls. Seated in front of the chariot are the Brahmin priests in charge. Above them are the elaborately carved figures of Skanda and Valli, which are decorated with garlands of flowers.

Kavadi and different groups of dancers who are unique to these celebrations are often accompanied by elephants and smaller illuminated chariots. The rich carnival atmosphere extends to the temple area, where traders of all kinds use the occasion to sell sugarcane juice, clothes, candies, brass utensils, and toys.

The Vel Festival is an entirely Hindu occasion, unlike the Kataragama Festival, which attracts people of various faiths from all over.

The extravagantly decorated Vel chariot is used to carry the weapons of Lord Skanda.

DEEPAVALI

Also known as the "Festival of Lights," Deepavali is a time of rejoicing for all Hindus. Thousands of oil lamps are lighted to celebrate the return of the exiled Lord Rama and to welcome Lakshmi, the Goddess of Wealth, into homes.

Deepavali is celebrated in November with intense fervor and gaiety by the young and old, rich and poor alike throughout Sri Lanka. The festival symbolizes the triumph of good over evil and a return of light into people's lives.

Although every state celebrates the occasion in its own special way, Deepavali is important because it shows the unity among the many groups of people in Sri Lanka.

Houses are always decorated with flickering earthen *diyas*, or oil lamps, during Deepavali, and the

During Deepavali houses are decorated with specially designed lamps of every kind.

day never goes by without the sound of bursting firecrackers in the streets. The lighting of lamps is the people's way of paying their respects to God for health, wealth, knowledge,

peace, valor, and fame. Everyone makes it a point to invite relatives, friends, and colleagues to their homes for rich feasts.

Deepavali is one time in the year that children

Children compete with one another to see who has the longest-burning sparkler.

happily get out of their beds before daybreak for their traditional oil baths at 3 A.M. After they are clean and dressed in their new festive attire, they begin the day's adventures by lighting little oil lamps, candles, and incense sticks in order to set off their firecrackers and sparklers. Competition can get quite stiff as each child races to set off the loudest or longest burning fireworks. The festival is also an especially enjoyable one for children since it is a day when adults are not supposed to say a single harsh word, so no one really gets told off for any minor wrongdoing.

Many believe that Deepavali is celebrated to mark the return of Lord Rama from his 14-year exile for a wrongfully punished sin. To commemorate his return to his kingdom, his subjects lighted the palace with thousands of oil lamps and set off firecrackers.

Another legend also has it that Goddess Lakshmi was so unhappy to have been separated from her beloved son, Vishnu, who was called to serve the god Brahman, that her grief affected the working of the entire universe. Lord Shiva then offered himself as a guard and pleaded with Brahman to relieve Vishnu, so that he could finally return to Lakshmi on the day of Deepavali. That is why it is believed that those who worship Goddess Lakshmi on this day would be given great riches.

Decorative figure of Goddess Lakshmi.

29

DURUTU PERAHERA

A major cultural festival held in Colombo, the Durutu Perahera, features a colorful pageant of elephants, dancers, and drummers.

The full moon in January is a very special occasion for Hindus in Sri Lanka.

This day, known as Durutu Poya, coincides with Buddha's first visit to Sri Lanka over twenty-five centuries ago. To remember his visit, an annual religious procession is held for three nights in Kelaniya, a town northeast of Colombo. The procession starts and ends at the Temple of Kelaniya. The festival consists of performances that show the country's cultural richness.

It is believed that Buddha first visited Sri Lanka nine months after his enlightenment. On that occasion he arrived at Mahiyangana, an ancient city west of Kandy, to restore peace among the warring Yakkha tribes. Buddha arrived in the beautiful Mahanaga Park just before the battle. The rival Yakkhas were all poised for battle when they noticed a stranger in yellow robes appearing in their midst. Many fled in fear into the jungles.

Later, they returned to listen to Buddha's message of peace. Having calmed down the Yakkhas, Buddha returned to India.

Although all this took place in Mahiyangana, the focus of the festival is on Kelaniya, which was blessed by Buddha on his third visit. Durutu Perahera draws thousands of spectators to watch the procession of ornamented elephants, torchbearers, dancers, and drummers march through the streets each night before going back to the temple.

WORDS TO KNOW

Abundance: A great or plentiful amount.

Astrologer: A person who practices astrology; one who professes to foretell events by the aspects and situation of the stars.

Betel: An evergreen Asian climbing shrub, which has oval leaves used to wrap cash gifts for Sinhala New Year.

Brahman: The Ultimate One among Hindu gods and goddesses.

Brahmin: A priest or a class of pious authorities who devote their lives to pursuing religious beliefs.

Devout: Devoted to religion.

Exorcist: A conjurer who can raise spirits.

Hinduism: A major religion in the Indian subcontinent.

Horoscopes: Astrological forecasts of people's futures.

Intricate: Having many complexly arranged elements.

Kavadi: An act of penance offered to Lord Skanda. It consists of carrying a decorated wooden arch in religious processions.

Kolam: The kolam is a good-fortune diagram drawn on thresholds of houses with rice powder.

Nirvana: The final state in which one has attained wisdom and compassion.

Pandal: A tent house made up of panels decorated with colorful images of deities.

Penance: An act of devotion performed voluntarily to show sorrow for a sin or other wrongdoing.

Reincarnation: Rebirth of the soul in another body.

Skanda: He is the god of war and disease, but he is also viewed as a protective deity by the Buddhists.

ACKNOWLEDGMENTS

WITH THANKS TO:
Krisinder Mukhtiar Kaur and Daphne Rodrigues for the loan of artifacts.

PHOTOGRAPHS BY:
Bes Stock (cover), John R. Jones (p. 10 top, p. 18 all, p. 20 both, p. 24, p. 26, p. 27 bottom left, p. 30), Yu Hui Ying (all other pictures)

ILLUSTRATIONS BY:
Cake (p. 1, pp. 4-5, p. 7, p. 25), Ong Lay Keng (p. 13), Lee Kowling (p. 23)

SET CONTENTS